"This wise and gentle book invites us to orient ourselves to awareness and wonder and gives us language, both traditional and contemporary, to express gratitude. It can serve as an aid to spiritual seekers and a resource for rabbis and teachers."

—**Rabbi Deborah Waxman**, President, Reconstructionist Rabbinical College

"This book is a bridge connecting the cultivation of gratitude to the treasure chest of Jewish blessings. It highlights blessings that have traditional places in the set liturgy and opens the possibility of using them to give voice to our gratitude—a blessing when resolving a conflict, a blessing to begin a community meeting, a blessing when hearing good news! Aided by this resource, a reader will be better able to discern and be grateful for moments of blessing."

—**Jacob Staub**, Professor of Jewish, Reconstructionist Rabbinical College

From Gratitude to Blessings and Back

From Gratitude to Blessings and Back

MARILYN PRICE
and
DAVID A. TEUTSCH

RESOURCE *Publications* · Eugene, Oregon

FROM GRATITUDE TO BLESSINGS AND BACK

Resource Publications
An Imprint of Wipf and Stock Publishers
199 W. 8th Ave., Suite 3
Eugene, OR 97401

www.wipfandstock.com

PAPERBACK ISBN: 978-1-5326-1771-3
HARDCOVER ISBN: 978-1-4982-4260-8
EBOOK ISBN: 978-1-4982-4259-2

Manufactured in the U.S.A.   SEPTEMBER 12, 2017

Contents

Acknowledgments

WE ARE GRATEFUL . . .

While writing a book on gratitude and its partner blessings, we would be remiss if we did not remember and honor the many people who brought us to the publication of this book.

From our beginnings we remember our parents and grandparents, who nurtured us, and those who taught us in formal settings, by mentoring and being mentored, and through friendship and love. In particular we are thankful for those who guide and love us daily, our spouses Betsy Teutsch and Roger Price and our children and their children, who provide us with hugs and countless other blessings.

We were blessed to have the help of Vivian Singer, of Custom Siddur, who helped us place the blessings in Hebrew font. Rabbi Michelle Greenfield did research to locate quotations from classical texts and modern sources that beautifully express wisdom that is relevant to our work.

To our editors and publishers at Wipf and Stock who guided us through to a finished book we are very grateful. They include Brian Palmer, James Stock, Jana Wipf, and Matthew Wimer, as well as our friend Rabbi Maurice Harris, who made the introductions that brought this book to print.

We are of course grateful to you the readers who choose to read this book and make the journey from gratitude to blessings and back. May your journey be a good one, and may it lead to many joys for you and our world.

ACKNOWLEDGMENTS

Just as Gratitude and Blessings are partners, so we are grateful and consider ourselves blessed to have had the opportunity to work with each other on this book. There was nothing but pleasure in its creation, and that is a blessing!

Thank you,
Marilyn and David

Chapter 1

A Conversation about Gratitude

WHEN I WAS LITTLE, my parents constantly reinforced the idea that hard work and self-discipline are the way to success. You obtain what you want by earning it. According to that set of beliefs, the world is a morally neutral place, and everything depends on you and what you make of it.

When I was little, my parents constantly reinforced the same ideals but with different language and undoubtedly different techniques. There is also no doubt that they told us, my brother and me, that we had to work to get what we wanted, and for sure they always underlined that it wasn't just up to us. It also depends on the things that are given us and on those who help us. So when I was little, I was taught to say "Thank you" every time something came my way. Gratitude overrode my hard work. I have clear memories not of prayers of thanksgiving to God but of thanksgiving to God's helpers on earth for making my dinner and walking me to school. It was not a neutral place at all, but a place where gratitude and thanks were modeled constantly.

My sense of the world as a neutral place was reinforced by the way I learned science. The world runs according to rules of nature that have no beginning and no end. Physics, chemistry and biology each have their own rules, and we can use scientific method to expand our knowledge of them. To do that, we maintain scientific neutrality.

The wonder that all small children have as they encounter the world around them can be replaced during childhood with a utilitarian take on the world and a sense of entitlement that flows from school, work, family, peers, and the media.

And then there is wonder! I have clear visions of marveling, even at the age of five, at the way I could skip because my very serious Grandpa Alex taught me—first one step and then another. I didn't connect the dots for a long time that the wonder of skipping and my body moving in mostly the right direction were not just about my accomplishments and what my grandpa taught me about trust and faith in him. Letting one foot leave the ground for a long time and not falling on my bottom required a different kind of faith, a trust. I remember very well when I accomplished that task. Hard work and discipline and wonder worked hand in hand.

Seeing the world as a place to be conquered, controlled and exploited is useful for getting ahead in a capitalist economy. Seeing the world as a place running on processes that can be rationally comprehended is critical for the advancement of science and technology. And that is how I came to see the world. I was good at getting ahead. But these two ways of looking at the world are quite joyless. As I moved into adulthood, it seemed to me that there must be more to life than that.

So here is where we begin, my partner in writing and I, to come to the same place only backwards. I started with wonder and then moved into God's realm. It wasn't that God wasn't there in my head, but God came later, and I was able to find a new place to give thanks. I began to connect the dots, so to speak. After a good meal prepared by my mom or a Sunday morning breakfast prepared by my dad, I could add God into the equation of thanks. It was richer, it was even more satisfying, and it was humbling. For with wonder comes the realization that we are not solely (soully) responsible for ourselves.

One piece fell in place when I read *Man Is Not Alone* and *God In Search of Man* by Rabbi Abraham Joshua Heschel while I was in college. What made a huge impression on me is the idea that the world is a wondrous place. I already knew that down deep inside me, but the thought had been driven out of my conscious mind by the conditioning that shaped my daily thinking. Catching onto that feeling of wonder helped me take a fresh look at what it means to be alive. The human body from that perspective is a totally astounding creation. And each of us has one!

When I was in college I studied art history and human anatomy working towards a degree in Medical Illustration (a task not completed), but the combination of those two introduced me to the intricacies of our bodies and their various expressions through the studies of anatomy and the different perspectives of the artist. The dissection of a body can make you gasp in great wonder, and seeing an artist's interpretation of the body quite simply made me sigh out loud and wonder how it all works. When I discovered the morning blessing for the body, it brought all that together in ways I never thought possible.

My body was a gift to me at birth. While my direct benefactors were my parents, there were doctors, nurses, and a hospital, and all my ancestors were involved as well. And the gifts just kept on coming—food, clothing, shelter, toys, and most of all, love and then later, teachers, professors—a fortune in education for which I paid only the tiniest fraction of the actual cost. And that education was based on centuries of cultural output, research and writing by a myriad of dedicated people. My life is based on an incalculable number of gifts. Many of them came from people I will never meet.

Medical researchers tell us that to thrive, babies need human touch and caring, that food and warmth are not enough. Franz Rosenzweig, A twentieth-century, German Jewish philosopher, wrote in his book, *A Star of Redemption*, that a child is gradually filled with its mother's love until that love overflows, which is when the child can begin to love its mother and then others. Our capacity to love is another of our invaluable gifts. For my mother to love me, she had to receive love from others first. We are part of a complex web of relationships that sustains our lives. And all those relationships are dependent on the natural world as well. As hard as I may work, I continue to receive vastly more than I could ever repay.

The attitude I have described above flows from wonder to awareness and culminates in gratitude. It is the attitude of gratitude that generates the feeling of gratitude.

Although it seems simple to those who understand and accept it, to have that great attitude is not so simple. Others understand it almost intuitively. Early one morning before a workshop I sat next to a woman, an early childhood educator from the inner city of Chicago, who was to become my student unbeknownst to me.

I turned and said, "Good morning." She responded in kind, and then I asked how she was this beautiful day, and she turned to me with a radiant smile and said, "Blessed." And she meant it. How she came to this great attitude of gratitude I do not know. But she had arrived, and I hope that we can duplicate this joy for you.

Chapter 2

Blessings over Food

Over grapes, grape juice, and wine:

בָּרוּךְ אַתָּה יהוה אֱלֹהֵינוּ מֶלֶךְ הָעוֹלָם בּוֹרֵא פְּרִי הַגָּפֶן:

Barukh ata Adonay eloheynu melekh ha'olam borey p'ri hagafen.

Blessed are you, Eternal One our God, the sovereign of all worlds who creates the fruit of the vine.

THIS BLESSING IS OFFERED solely in gratitude for the fruit of the vine. When wine is used for sanctification, as on Shabbat and holidays and at weddings, a second blessing is devoted to sanctifying the occasion. When wine or grape juice is used at a wedding or for Kiddush on Shabbat, it is customary to fill the cup to overflowing because wine is a symbol of joy in Jewish tradition.

When Matt got married, we were fortunate to have his uncle, my brother who was a rabbi, perform the ceremony. He had given me much good advice throughout my life, and on this most special of days he had told me to only watch the young couple during the ceremony and not the community so that I would always remember their expressions and love for each other at that moment. Because I was so focused on them, I didn't see the expression of distress on my brother's face when he noticed that no one had remembered to put wine in the wine cup! With an actor's aplomb he made sure that the couple pretended to drink the wine, which was clearly not overflowing although their love surely was and is.

A folk tale: Whenever there was a celebration in a village, everyone was invited. Often the host would ask the people to share the responsibility for bringing the food or wine. On this particular occasion everyone was asked to bring a cask of wine and pour it into a large container so that there would be enough for everyone to share. The villagers did as they were asked, or so it seemed. When the time came for the toast, they were astonished to find that the container was filled with water. Rather than share their precious wine, everyone thought that the others would bring wine so that their contribution of water would go unnoticed. A joyous celebration needs the full participation of all those in attendance!

The sensations of wine! After a toast, it is customary to click the glasses together. Why do we click? It is a sensory matter of course. We can smell the fragrance of the wine, we can see it, we can touch it, and we can taste it, but we can't hear it. So in order to use all of our senses, we click the glasses together and say "*l'chayim*," to life in all its sensations. In doing so, we affirm the community's support for the toast.

Rabbi Wolf Zitomirer was a village innkeeper. A Jewish customer came in and ordered a glass of brandy. When he was about to drink it without reciting a blessing, the rabbi stopped him and said, "Do you realize the miracles through which God has produced the fruit of the vine that became the drink you are about to enjoy? And you have forgotten to offer God even a brief blessing." The customer promptly recited the blessing, and the rabbi answered, "Amen."

—*Adapted from* Me'orot G'dolot, 2, 26a

Over bread and the diverse foods of a major meal:

בָּרוּךְ אַתָּה יהוה אֱלֹהֵינוּ מֶלֶךְ הָעוֹלָם הַמּוֹצִיא לֶחֶם מִן הָאָרֶץ:

Barukh ata Adonay eloheynu melekh haʼolam hamotzi lechem min haʼaretz.

Blessed are you, Eternal One our God, the sovereign of all worlds who brings forth bread from the earth.

WHY DOESN'T THIS BLESSING say, "who brings forth wheat from the earth?" Because we are not only grateful for the sun, rain, soil, and seed. We are grateful for the farmer and the baker. Gratitude for bread requires recognition of the divine-human partnership.

I think of this blessing as the slow-down-and-remember blessing. We often rush to the table. Multiple reasons exist for why we rush to eat. Sometimes we don't even wait for everyone to get to the table and join us. We not only rush to the table, but we also rush our eating, and again we forget this precious gift of having food to eat. This blessing provides a pause for remembering.

We were seated in a crowded and bustling restaurant in Atlanta, Georgia, and a particularly lovely couple was seated across the aisle from us. They were clearly enjoying each other's company and delighting in getting to know each other. I treated myself to many sideward looks at them to capture their glow. When their meal came, they joined hands and, looking at each other, took many minutes to say thank you. Perhaps the thank you extended beyond the bread they blessed and included the time spent with each other, and perhaps the blessing extended beyond themselves and the bread. It certainly included God. It is good to remember that this blessing over the sustenance of our lives, and bread in particular, includes God.

Ben Zoma used to say: How much labor Adam must have expended before he obtained bread to eat! He ploughed, sowed, reaped, piled up the sheaves, threshed, winnowed, selected the grain, ground and sifted the flour, kneaded and baked, and after that he ate. By contrast, I get up in the morning and find all this prepared for me. And how much labor must Adam have expended before he obtained a garment to wear! He sheared and washed the wool, combed and spun it, wove, and after that he obtained a garment to wear. By contrast, I get up in the morning and find all this prepared for me. All artisans attend and come to the door of my house, and I get up and find all these things before me.

—TALMUD *BERAKHOT* 58A

Over baked goods other than bread:

בָּרוּךְ אַתָּה יהוה אֱלֹהֵינוּ מֶלֶךְ הָעוֹלָם בּוֹרֵא מִינֵי מְזוֹנוֹת:

Barukh ata Adonay eloheynu melekh haolam borey miney m'zonot.

Blessed are you, Eternal One our God, the sovereign of all worlds who creates various kinds of foods.

DESSERT IS ONE OF my favorite luxuries, especially if it involves chocolate. For many, the use of sugar and eggs makes buying dessert a rare splurge. For others, watching weight or cholesterol or sugar intake puts dessert into the category of a special treat. I, for one, never take a brownie for granted! Adding a blessing reminds us to appreciate the moment.

I believe that the recipes we carry down the deepest in our hearts and our memories are baked goods. I have vivid memories not just of the taste of my mom's plum cake but my grandma Mabelle's mandel brot, my friend Joe's just about anything chocolate, and one particular recipe from my cousin Helen called "Helen's What." I can see the plates they were served on, the smells they evoked, the smiles, and the way they tasted each time I have the opportunity to revisit them. Because all of the above original chefs are now gone, it is up to me to recreate these recipes so that they live on. Sometimes when I make them, I am successful, and sometimes, but not every time, they recreate a wonderful connection with the chefs of old, and that moment has a special flavor all of its own.

One of the worst bakers I loved was my mother-in-law. She was the best of humans, and her greatest joys were to care for her beloveds. I knew what to ask her to bring to the table when she came for feasts. These were things she had been making for years, and they were steady and within her skills. Yet she often wanted to try baking something whose recipe she had read. Of course we encouraged her, and she persevered. The cake always came with one corner cut out of the side. When that first happened, I was convinced that she had burned it or dropped the pan, but before I could even ask, she assured me that the cake was good because she had tried it—and lived! There is a blessing over baked goods other than bread, and it is also a blessing to remember the baker.

Over fruit that grows on trees:

בָּרוּךְ אַתָּה יהוה אֱלֹהֵינוּ מֶלֶךְ הָעוֹלָם בּוֹרֵא פְּרִי הָעֵץ:

Barukh ata Adonay eloheynu melekh ha'olam borey p'ri ha'etz.

Blessed are you, Eternal One our God, the sovereign of all worlds who creates the fruit of the tree.

MOST OF US CITY dwellers do not grow our own fruit. Our children often don't know what grows on a soft vine like cantaloupes, what grows in the earth like potatoes, and what grows in trees like apples and peaches. The food blessings that separate among these categories remind us to look beyond what comes to our kitchen from the market to the farmer, sun, soil, and rain. Tree fruits cannot be harvested in the year a sapling is planted. Patience and care must accompany nature and nurture for us to have a bite of luscious fruit.

We moved into our urban house outside of Chicago in February, and everything was covered with snow. In April we discovered seven fruit trees in the backyard. It was not as glamorous as I make it sound, as many of them had no business being planted in this climate, but they were lovely to watch. First came the flowers on the pear tree and then the four apple trees and one cherry and then the oddest one of all, a multi-grafted fruit tree that was supposed to give us apricots and plums. Watching the trees blossom and then fruit was as valuable a lesson for the then babies, my human saplings, in the household as then watching the products of those misplaced trees be harvested for possible jellies and really bad applesauce and then watching the leaves and their rebirth. The trees are now gone except for the stubborn pear tree that after 43 years still helps to mark the seasons and the time.

> If you see bread and say, "Blessed is the One who created this bread; how nice this bread is," that counts as a blessing. If you see figs and say, "Blessed is the One who created these figs," that counts as a blessing as well.
>
> —RABBI MEIR, *TOSEFTA B'RAKHOT* 4.5

Over fruits and vegetables that grow in soil:

בָּרוּךְ אַתָּה יהוה אֱלֹהֵינוּ מֶלֶךְ הָעוֹלָם בּוֹרֵא פְּרִי הָאֲדָמָה:

Barukh ata Adonay eloheynu melekh ha'olam borey p'ri ha'adama.

Blessed are you, Eternal One our God, the sovereign of all worlds who creates the fruit of the earth.

UNLESS I AM REALLY thinking about it, I often don't consider the fact that french fries are a form of potato. The same with munching on potato chips. Connecting prepared foods with their raw form is a natural thing for a cook to do, but when I do not cook, I usually enjoy the aesthetics of the presentation of the food at the table and lose track of where it comes from, in this case, out of the earth. There is a Yiddish curse that says, "May you grow like an onion, with your head in the ground." But of course that is not a curse for the onion. Amazing that brilliantly colored radishes and carrots emerge full-grown from the dirt! This blessing reminds us of some very tasty everyday miracles.

There is a big difference between stretching up to reach the fruit from trees and kneeling on the ground to plant and dig and then harvest the fruits and vegetables that grow in the soil. Rudyard Kipling wrote in his poem "The Glory of the Garden" that more than half of Adam the gardener's work was done upon his knees. The poem goes on to say that when the work was finished, Adam would wash his hands and pray. If you have ever planted either from seed or from a seedling and then tended and watched the plant grow; if you have ever waited for the rain to fall or covered your plants to protect them from the cold or peeked under the ground to see if they are ready only to discover it is too soon; if you have watched in amazement when the "fruit" of your labor becomes the fruit on your table, then you have experienced a wonder. If you, the gardener or the eater, have done any of those things or eaten anything fresh from the garden, then your prayers of gratitude should be a little sweeter, especially after you wash your hands.

It is well established that Jews offer blessings. It is the case with all enjoyment of the world, that when we offer a blessing, we connect the divine to our enjoyment. God then becomes more present in our lives.

—Rabbi Judah Aryeh Leib,
S'fat Emet, Masechet B'rakhot, 35a

On other foods and beverages:

בָּרוּךְ אַתָּה יהוה אֱלֹהֵינוּ מֶלֶךְ הָעוֹלָם שֶׁהַכֹּל נִהְיֶה בִּדְבָרוֹ:

Barukh ata Adonay eloheynu melekh ha'olam she'hakol niyeh bidvaro.

Blessed are you, Eternal One our God, the sovereign of all worlds whose word shapes what can be.

CONTEMPORARY PREPARED FOODS USUALLY have many ingredients. Frequently the ingredients by themselves would receive different blessings. Often a food does not look like the individual ingredients did when they entered the factory or kitchen. In both of those cases, a different blessing is said. While it is the food preparer who has created something new, it is still attributed to the Divine. That is so not only because of the origin of the principal ingredients. It is because we can only do what the laws of nature allow. Human creativity operates within the structure of the universe that predates the emergence of human life.

While there is no particular blessing, except this one, for inventions in the areas of food preparation and ease for the contemporary lifestyle, this would win my prize for the ways in which the busiest of us are given the opportunity to quickly and easily present a meal for a family of any size. This blessing recalls for me my favorite treat as a kid when my parents went out, the frozen TV dinner. The clever and careful way that the designer made sections of my dinner was inspiring to my young and eager mind. My brother and I would happily devour the prepackaged meals and of course save the containers for some art project. I don't remember if we even had a TV, but we certainly had the meal and were grateful for it!

Some things deserve their own blessings: (The standard ones never seem to do.) Like fresh sheets or chocolate milk or taking a ride through a car wash on a sunny afternoon so it won't rain on the clean car. Or a cup of coffee standing alert in a cheerful mug greeting me at breakfast, or a glass of iced coffee with the milk sliding between the cubes like white banners against the dark sky, or a cup of decaf with cream and sugar after dinner. Rich enough to replace dessert, but kind enough to let me sleep. Some things, not everything, but some things deserve their own blessings: like strong coffee, fresh bagels, homemade jam, preferably fig, and you.

—RABBI LEWIS JOHN ERON

Who is rich? Those who take pleasure in their lot, as it says, "When you eat as a result of your efforts, you will be happy." (Psalms 128:2)

—BEN ZOMA, *MISHNA AVOT* 4.1

At the end of a meal:

בָּרוּךְ אַתָּה יהוה אֱלֹהֵינוּ מֶלֶךְ הָעוֹלָם הַזָן אֶת הַכֹּל:

Barukh ata Adonay eloheynu melekh haolam hazan et hakol.

Blessed are you, Eternal One our God, the sovereign of all worlds who sustains all.

THE TORAH SAYS, "YOU shall eat, become satisfied and then offer blessing." (Deuteronomy 8:10) Many religious traditions say a blessing before meals, but what do we make of the request that we bless afterward? When we are satisfied, it is easy to take full credit for all we have and all we are. Self-satisfaction is a source of spiritual blindness. Offering a blessing after a meal helps us fight smugness.

After every family meal growing up, we had several responsibilities. The first one was to thank my mom for dinner. This was not optional. The second was to help clean up. That was not optional either. My brother and I took turns with the chores. One of us did the dishes, and one of us dried them. I learned early on that being satisfied with food carried a price. I also knew that the camaraderie of conversation and the partnership of cleanup were valuable in making us part of the process.

We never said the traditional blessing because in our secular Jewish home, we had no idea there was one. When we eventually went to the Reform synagogue across the street, we learned of blessings but not the blessings after the meal, as such blessings were not common in Reform congregations in those days. When I learned about this amazing blessing, it took on many forms in my head and around many different tables. I still like to think of it as another chance to remember the source (mom and God), take a breath and go about the business of life stronger and more connected.

And you shall eat and be satisfied, and bless the Eternal One our God for the good land which God has given us. Beware lest you forget the Eternal One our God, in not keeping God's commandments, ordinances, and statutes, which have been commanded to you today; and lest when you have eaten and are satisfied, and have built goodly houses and live in them ... that your ego swell up and you forget the Eternal One our God, who brought us forth out of the land of Egypt, out of the house of bondage ... and you say in your heart: "My power and the might of my hand have brought me this wealth." (Deuteronomy 8:10)

At the end of a meal—a second blessing:

בָּרוּךְ אַתָּה יהוה אֱלֹהֵינוּ מֶלֶךְ הָעוֹלָם עַל הָאָרֶץ וְעַל הַמָּזוֹן:

Barukh ata Adonay eloheynu melekh ha'olam al ha'aretz v'al hamazon.

Blessed are you, Eternal One our God, the sovereign of all worlds for the land and the food.

EVERYTHING I EAT EITHER comes from the store, with someone else usually then cooking it, or from a restaurant kitchen. I give thanks to the Source of rain, sun and soil. No less, I am grateful to the farmers, truckers, store-keepers, cooks, and wait staff who provide food that is nutritious and also delicious.

Our interdependence only works because of a high level of trust in our complex exchanges. This gives me hope that we can find fairer and more peaceful ways to share the land and its produce. Gratitude provides a path to mutual caring and support.

Without getting into the politics of the fine art of tipping, we know that it is the common way of thanking wait staff and others who give us service. Tipping reminds me of the difference between my concept of a good tip and the one of the generation before that. My parents (and my in-laws) were wonderful and generous people in their praise and in their deeds, but none of them quite got the tipping process. My dad would make the waiters his best friends, joke with them and make them feel wonderful. When we finished the meal and thanked those who had helped us, which might include a trip to the kitchen to thank the chef, he would pay the bill and leave a tip. His typical tip, no matter the cost of the bill, was one dollar. He was the best customer but the worst tipper. As soon as the coast was clear and he couldn't see what I was doing, I would race back to the table and add some money to his standard tip. As cheap as his actions may seem to most, for him it was not about money, and if you asked any one of the many people who took care of him then and later in life, they would tell you that his level of gratitude was the best. Thanking God the provider should be the biggest tip of all.

The commandment to offer a blessing after meals was interwoven into the life of traditional Jews through the words they said at the end of every meal. Offering this blessing turns enjoying food into an opportunity to remind ourselves of its Source.

—RABBI SAMSON RAPHAEL HIRSCH,
COMMENTARY ON DEVARIM 8:10

Chapter 3

Blessings for Nature

On seeing the ocean:

בָּרוּךְ אַתָּה יהוה אֱלֹהֵינוּ מֶלֶךְ הָעוֹלָם שֶׁעָשָׂה אֶת הַיָם הַגָּדוֹל:

Barukh ata Adonay eloheynu melekh ha'olam she'asa et hayam hagadol.

Blessed are you, Eternal One our God, the sovereign of all worlds who made the great sea.

WHEN I WAS LITTLE, our family sometimes went to the beach on summer vacations. I never tired of watching the waves, of the feel of sand under my feet and of the surf's endless pushing and pulling. I quickly learned that the tides and waves had to do with gravitational pull from the sun and moon, but the scientific facts had no influence on the mesmerizing power of the waves. Seeing the beach each morning was an awe-inspiring experience. Wonder and science operate on different planes of our existence. Listen to the crashing surf! See the sun glint on the water! Feel a power far beyond our own.

I am sitting by the window overlooking the Pacific Ocean. The wind is howling, and the rain has been nonstop for hours. In my chair with my cup of orange tea warm and fragrant next to me, I feel safe. But the ocean, restless and breathless, is threatening and fascinating.

Yesterday walking along the shore, watching the sunset, seeing the birds perch and fly and the kids play on the then calm ocean, I felt exhilarated yet safe. The ocean—like people—changes.

Powerful, predictable, unstable, changing! Pleasure bringing and danger making! Filled with life and death. Can you connect this power with God and people's changing nature? How can you not.

On the other side of the country I am privileged to sit by the Atlantic watching the waves crash along the shore while on a week's vacation. I am thinking of my ancestors travelling over it toward this land over 100 years ago. As big and endless as it looks to me, I can't imagine my grandma Elisheva's angst and also excitement as she headed from her Romanian homeland with one little girl toward a life with so much mystery and so many possibilities. If this massive tumultuous ocean is mysterious and powerful to me, I cannot begin to imagine how it was for her and the brave others as they headed to this land of freedom. I imagine her prayers were delivered in Romanian with a fervor that matched her fears and her joys.

On seeing a rainbow:

בָּרוּךְ אַתָּה יהוה אֱלֹהֵינוּ מֶלֶךְ הָעוֹלָם זוֹכֵר הַבְּרִית וְנֶאֱמָן בִּבְרִיתוֹ וְקַיָּם בְּמַאֲמָרוֹ׃

Barukh ata Adonay eloheynu melekh ha'olam zokher habrit v'ne'eman bivrito v'kayam b'ma'aro.

Blessed are you, Eternal One our God, the sovereign of all worlds who remembers the covenant, remains faithful to it, and fulfills its word.

WE HAVE BEEN LISTENING to and singing songs about rainbows for as long as there have been songs. In 1939 Isidore Hochberg (Edgar Yipsel "Yip" Harburg) and Harold Arlen wrote the music and the lyrics for the Wizard of Oz, which included the hit sung by Judy Garland, "Somewhere over the Rainbow." Harburg the lyricist was known for the social commentary of his lyrics as well as his liberal sensibilities. The song speaks of the good on the other side of the prophetic rainbow. When you remember what was happening in the war-torn world of 1939, this particular poignant piece of music is even more striking. Because rainbows appear seemingly out of nowhere after the storm (scientific explanations aside), they are quite magical and do evoke wonder. Later on, another song was written and sung by a puppet named Kermit the Frog, who asked the question, "Why are there so many songs about rainbows, and what's on the other side?" Rainbows promise that even the worst shall pass and that the sun will shine. Good lessons.

According to Genesis, God sent a rainbow after the Flood as a signal of God's promise not to flood the whole world again. The colorful arc often marks the end of a storm. It reminds us that even the fiercest storm will pass.

On seeing beautiful trees:

בָּרוּךְ אַתָּה יהוה אֱלֹהֵינוּ מֶלֶךְ הָעוֹלָם שֶׁלֹּא חִסַּר בְּעוֹלָמוֹ כְּלוּם וּבָרָא בּוֹ בְּרִיּוֹת טוֹבוֹת
וְאִילָנוֹת טוֹבִים לְהַנּוֹת בָּהֶם בְּנֵי אָדָם:

Barukh ata Adonay eloheynu melekh ha'olam shelo chiser b'olamo davar uvara vo b'riyot tovot v'ilanot tovim l'hanot bahem b'ney adam.

Blessed are you, Eternal One our God, the sovereign of all worlds who has withheld nothing from our world and has created beautiful creatures and goodly trees for people to enjoy.

How wonderful to bask in the shade of a big oak tree on a hot, sunny day! How the holly glows green in my snowy yard in midwinter. The leafing of the trees in spring is a harbinger of better things to come. And the trees' leaves glowing yellow, orange and red in autumn always make me smile.

One of my favorite folk tales tells the story of a little girl who lives in a village in a valley nestled at the base of a tree-lined hill. Every day, so the story goes, the men and boys go out and hunt for dinner while the women climb the hill to find wood to keep the fire going. They do not use the wood from the trees on their hill but climb and find branches beyond. This is a daily trip, and the young girl goes obediently, but finally one day she asks her mother why they can't use the wood near their home. Her mother patiently explains that those trees are their protectors and friends, and that their roots go deep into the ground and make sure that the village is secure when the rain comes and that the villagers can sit under the trees in the shade when the sun beats down. The girl accepts that, as she knows it is true. The routine continues until one day on their way up the hill, she notices that men have come to their small village carrying axes and heading for the trees. She runs toward them and tells them they must go away and not chop down the trees, that the trees are their friends and give them shade and protection. They laugh at her and continue on their way. With a great deal of courage, she quickly calls out to her friends in the village that they must each pick a tree and hug it and not to let go, and they do. With the children's arms wrapped around the trees on the hill, the men turn and leave. The children, taking matters into their own hands (and arms), save the trees, the trees that give life and protect it.

Over natural wonders:

בָּרוּךְ אַתָּה יהוה אֱלֹהֵינוּ מֶלֶךְ הָעוֹלָם עוֹשֶׂה מַעֲשֵׂה בְרֵאשִׁית:

Barukh ata Adonay eloheynu melekh haolam oseh maaseh v'reyshit.

Blessed are you, Eternal One our God, the sovereign of all worlds, author of creation.

EVEN THE MOST JADED of us is occasionally thunderstruck by the sight of a night sky illuminated by stars, or the vista from high on a mountain, or waves crashing on an empty beach, or a tree backlit by a stunning sunset. And sometimes it is something beautiful if not quite so thunderous: raindrops on a leaf, a tiny wildflower, a horse grazing in a meadow. Such wondrous moments deserve to be treasured; they are gifts that remind us of our smallness amidst the world's grandeur.

Driving to the airport in Philadelphia from a camp where I was working farther south, I brushed against the hints of spring. Because of the late arrival of the season, everything seemed to have popped at once. The daffodils, hyacinths, tulips all were blooming. It was almost too much to take in. The green haze surrounding the trees was just ready to leaf and make it all official. I felt that I could barely wait but knew that I should try to slow down and make it last longer.

This was for me a teachable moment, and this is what I learned: We need to cultivate the ability to enjoy the now and not constantly look into the future. Many of us are guilty of this. Always looking forward to the next best thing, the best is next to come, all will be better when it (whatever *it* is) happens. . . .

Don't get me wrong. To anticipate is a good thing, especially when the now is problematic or actually even when the now is beautiful . . . like seeing tulips, daffodils, hyacinths and magnolia bushes all at the same time. Who couldn't enjoy that? When the now is beautiful, we need to give thanks for it.

Rabbi Levi commented upon the apparent contradiction between two biblical verses. One says, "The world and all that it contains belongs to God." The other verse says, "The heavens belong to God, but the earth God gave to people." He resolved the contradiction by stating that one verse refers to the world before one offers a blessing, and the other after its recitation.

—BABYLONIAN TALMUD, *B'RAKHOT* 35A

On seeing shooting stars or lightning or hearing thunder:

בָּרוּךְ אַתָּה יהוה אֱלֹהֵינוּ מֶלֶךְ הָעוֹלָם שֶׁכֹּחוֹ וּגְבוּרָתוֹ מָלֵא עוֹלָם:

Barukh ata Adonay eloheynu melekh ha'olam shekocho ug'vurato maley olam.

Blessed are you, Eternal One our God, the sovereign of all worlds whose power and might fill the world.

BEING HUMAN MAKES US small parts of a vast universe. In our day-to-day lives, most of us lose track of that reality amidst the focus on working with colleagues, getting jobs done, performing chores and capitalizing on recreational opportunities. Then a clap of thunder or powerful storm reminds us of the power and majesty of the world, and for a moment we awaken to that greater reality.

Shooting stars, lightning, and thunder are magnificent acts of nature to be honored. But it turns out that a shooting star is not a star at all, but a meteor heading to earth. Lightning can be dangerous albeit beautiful, and thunder warns us that lightning might be near. Long ago I learned a trick. If you count the seconds between the lightning and the thunder, as in "one hippopotamus, two hippopotamus," and so on, you know how many miles away the lightning has struck. As the number gets higher, people's fear diminishes. I have used the counting trick to reduce a variety of other fears as well. When we put aside our fears, those scientific acts of wonder connect us to God.

On seeing something of natural beauty:

בָּרוּךְ אַתָּה יהוה אֱלֹהֵינוּ מֶלֶךְ הָעוֹלָם שֶׁכָּכָה לוֹ בְּעוֹלָמוֹ:

Barukh ata Adonay eloheynu melekh haʼolam sheʼkakha lo bʼolamo.

Blessed are you, Eternal One our God, the sovereign of all worlds whose universe contains such things.

HIKING IN YOSEMITE NATIONAL Park, I emerged from the forest and found myself on an outcropping with Yosemite Falls glistening across the valley from me. It was too far away for the sound of the water to reach me, but it was a breathtaking sight framed by forest and rock. That waterfall demanded wonder, and who could not obey?

Beau-ti-ful adj. 1. Having qualities that delight the senses, especially the sense of sight. 2. Excellent; wonderful. A dictionary definition does not help to define beauty. It is as personal and subjective and as open to criticism as any concept could possibly be. What is beautiful to some is definitely not beautiful to others. This blessing in particular reminds me of the aphorism, "Beauty is in the eyes of the beholder," reminding us to look deeper than the external to find the beauty that God has planted within, calls us to natural beauty and urges us to dig for the values of the people we include in our blessings.

I heard a story of a woman who became a grandmother for the first time. Her family wanted to know what the baby should eventually call her. She replied, "Beautiful, no one has ever called me beautiful." And so she is!

Upon looking at the night sky:

בָּרוּךְ אַתָּה יהוה אֱלֹהֵינוּ מֶלֶךְ הָעוֹלָם יוֹצֵר הַמְּאוֹרוֹת:

Barukh ata Adonay eloheynu melekh ha'olam yotzer ham'orot.

Blessed are you, Eternal One our God, the sovereign of all worlds shaper of the heavens' lights.

ON BACKPACKING TRIPS WE used to make camp many miles from the nearest road. Staring upward at night, the stars were so bright that it seemed possible to reach up and touch them. The moon was a giant, glowing orb. The beauty was mesmerizing. The Milky Way is always spread out overhead, waiting for us to look up and see the stars.

There is a star twinkling immediately over my head, a quite remarkable thing to see. To experience. To be a part of. If one relaxes enough into the experience, other stars join in, each brighter than the other. Then the crescent moon slides in. What really pulls it all together is that I can see it, and those nowhere near me can see it as well. If we are looking at the same thing, does that connect us? Does the power of that connection recall the faith that pulls us together? Is there a blessing for that wonder? Naturally there is!

I love the moon. I find her comings and goings and changing of sizes personally satisfying. Her folktales and myths are a story listener and teller's delight. One of my favorites is the story of a princess who feels empathy for the moon, who keeps changing sizes. The princess wants to find the perfect material that will stretch to fit the moon when she is at her fullest and shrink when she is at her smallest. The call goes out to the kingdom to find the perfect material, and as tales go, hundreds of fabric merchants and tailors try to satisfy the beloved princess's request, but none can be found except by the wisest person. She is not particularly prominent. I have always believed that would be a grandmother. She takes the princess aside and tells her, "Such a material does not exist, but the moon is dressed in the clouds and the stars, and the admiration from the people on earth is indeed her closet, as she sees reflected in them the love and glow that clothes." I think it is on the days when the moon is at her fullest and brightest that the love is strongest.

In celebration of living things:

בָּרוּךְ אַתָּה יהוה אֱלֹהֵינוּ מֶלֶךְ הָעוֹלָם מְחַיֵּה כָּל־חָי:

Barukh ata Adonay eloheynu melekh ha'olam m'chayey kol chay.

Blessed are you, Eternal One our God, the sovereign of all worlds who gives life to all that lives.

AT THE ZOO a little girl was peering gleefully at an elephant. Before long, she was distracted by a pigeon walking at her feet. Who is to say which animal is the more remarkable? The diversity of sizes, shapes, colors and diets seems endless. The future of creaturely diversity depends on us because of the impact that we have on our environment. Humans can help preserve animal and plant species by restricting damage to natural habitats and reversing global warming. The determination to act begins with appreciation for our fellow creatures.

Early on in the summer our four year-old grandson's preschool class watched the development of a caterpillar to a butterfly. They witnessed the creation of a cocoon and then the emerging of a butterfly and then its eventual flight in subsequent celebration. I am a particular fan of these seemingly fragile flyers as they change from relatively unattractive caterpillars (unless you're another caterpillar) into ethereally delicate butterflies. I watch them in amazement as they flit from flower to flower with little effort and much beauty.

Then one morning I witnessed another metamorphosis as I watched Hazel asleep in my arms swaddled from chin to toe in a cocoon of her own. Protected in her man-made cocoon, she is developing into the woman she will become. These coverings in many ways are quite similar—they protect externally and allow internal processes to do their job. We don't know exactly what will emerge, but we do know that each is carefully protected in its own way.

The wonders of nature have long been blessed by Judaism: The blessing above fits a variety of occasions. It connects us to the eyes of a four year-old watching a caterpillar become a butterfly and then setting it free, and it connects us to the gentle effective swaddling of a baby, a different kind of creation.

At dusk:

בָּרוּךְ אַתָּה יהוה אֱלֹהֵינוּ מֶלֶךְ הָעוֹלָם הַמַּעֲרִיב עֲרָבִים:

Barukh ata Adonay eloheynu melekh ha'olam hama'ariv aravim.

Blessed are you, Eternal One our God, the sovereign of all worlds who brings on the evening.

Most peoples of the world see the day as starting at sunup and continuing through the night. Jews calculate the day from sunset to sunset, with the evening marking the beginning of the new day. Jews start with the dark, often associated with danger, and proceed toward the light.

Dusk occurs at the darkest stage of twilight, or at the very end of astronomical twilight after sunset and just before night. The word itself evokes a dim, dark space filled with mystery and, for some, romance. It is as dark as it can be and still have a glimmer of light, enough to see shadows but not clearly. Dusk is also when the most beautiful aftereffects of a sunset can be seen. Unable to let it all go, the sun casts remarkable glimmering light that radiates especially on lake or ocean waters. Sometimes the after-sets are more spectacular than the sunsets. Dusk is the final curtain of the fading day. In the days before electric lighting, using the day's last natural light could be a harried time just before the quiet of the dark. Yes, dusk describes itself very well. It is at once shadowy, romantic, harried and mysterious. With dusk comes gratitude for a new day.

When recognizing the unity of all creation:

בָּרוּךְ אַתָּה יהוה אֱלֹהֵינוּ מֶלֶךְ הָעוֹלָם יוֹצֵר אוֹר וּבוֹרֵא חֹשֶׁךְ עֹשֶׂה שָׁלוֹם וּבוֹרֵא אֶת־הַכֹּל:

Barukh ata Adonay eloheynu melekh ha'olam yotzer or uvorey choshekh oseh shalom uvorey et hakol.

Blessed are you, Eternal One our God, the sovereign of all worlds who creates light and darkness, makes peace and creates all that is.

OUR SURVIVAL DEPENDS UPON our ability to benefit from our environment, which often requires us to alter it. That is what tools are all about. Focusing on the pieces we need to use, we concentrate on the things that can improve our lives. In the process, we can easily forget to step back and see the big picture—the unity of all that is. When a glimpse of that totality brings us back to greater awareness, it is time to offer a blessing.

I love the entire experience of flying, but what I most love is sitting all cozy in the window seat, looking out and seeing the world! Driving or walking on the ground, I try to see as much of the environs as I can. But there I see little compared to soaring in a plane above the sky and watching the world pass under my feet. I become quite literally overwhelmed with the wonder of it. From a distance I can imagine that the world is one, and on long flights I can watch the sun set and see lights from houses and cars going down roads. On a wintry day the ground is often covered with snow, and in the fall nature's paintbrush shapes a wonderful blaze of color. I can only imagine what all of creation looks like from the spaceships that fly up and beyond, catching it all in one breathtaking view. That is the all, a world worth a blessing.

Chapter 4

Blessings Related to the Five Senses

On smelling spices or fragrances:

בָּרוּךְ אַתָּה יהוה אֱלֹהֵינוּ מֶלֶךְ הָעוֹלָם בּוֹרֵא מִינֵי בְשָׂמִים:

Barukh ata Adonay eloheynu melekh ha'olam borey miney v'samim.

Blessed are you, Eternal One our God, the sovereign of all worlds who creates a variety of spices.

THERE ARE BLESSINGS TO celebrate each of our senses: light for the eyes, food for taste, sounds for hearing, clothes for touching, and spices for smell. If we are attentive, we can find blessing—and an opportunity to encounter grace—often during every day.

Scents are a wonderful link to our memories. Garlic in the hallways of my grandma Libby's apartment building, the spices of Havdalah and Desitin from my babies.

Many Shabbat afternoons we would take three buses crosstown and arrive at my Grandma and Grandpa Lebovitz's Westside Chicago apartment. Surrounded with big wordless hugs and intimate smells of garlic and Romanian food-love that was the Shabbat of my kid-hood. Grandma Libby had a few interesting no's for Shabbat. We were not allowed to play cards or sew, but we could take the bus to her house, and we absolutely had to eat everything on our plates. That was garlic love at Grandma's house.

Havdalah spices are famous. We bless the sweet smell of Shabbat and say goodbye, bringing the sweetness into the week. I remember one particular Shabbat afternoon on an Adult Learning Retreat walking through an herb garden and picking fresh rosemary for the spice box. All recipes that call for rosemary bring me back to that walk.

And then there's Desitin. For any parent, grandparent or anyone who was ever a kid (did I leave anyone out?) there is the smell of Desitin ointment. Principally it is used as an impenetrable sealer for all bad things on a baby's sweet bottom, so the smell is poignant and reminiscent of time spent with little ones. As I cuddled little Hazel this morning before we left for the airport, I took deep breaths of this most unusual and memorable odor and the sweet baby smell that comes with all babies. We left for the airport, and I cherished that sweet smell for longer than I thought possible.

Then I glanced down at the lovely silk shirt I was wearing and learned why. Sweet Hazel Juliet in her desire to have me remember her had left a smear of Desitin across a very noticeable part of my shirt. In spite of all my noblest of efforts, the impenetrable Desitin remains. I wear that shirt with a smile.

On seeing a flame:

בָּרוּךְ אַתָּה יהוה אֱלֹהֵינוּ מֶלֶךְ הָעוֹלָם בּוֹרֵא מְאוֹרֵי הָאֵשׁ:

Barukh ata Adonay eloheynu melekh ha'olam borey m'orey ha'esh.

Blessed are you, Eternal One our God, the sovereign of all worlds who creates the light of fire.

In the early development of our species, fire not only warmed us in winter and provided the means to cook food that would otherwise have been inedible, it also lit up the dark. The human fascination with flame has extended throughout our history. The flame can be a powerful work tool or an invitation to romance or a symbol of truth, but never something to be taken for granted.

Gathering around a campfire and watching the flames is mesmerizing. Sitting by the fireplace on a cold wintery day is cozy and relaxing. The warmth of the fire is therapeutic when it is in the right place, and a properly placed fire can be gentle and well used.

My grandpa Al made up wonderful stories for us when we were little, and he often started like this: The men were gathered around the campfire, and they asked their lieutenant to tell them a story, and he did. It went like this:
The men were gathered around the campfire, and they asked their lieutenant to tell them a story, and he did. It went like this:
The men were gathered around the campfire, and they asked their lieutenant to tell them a story, and he did. It went like this:
And on and on he would go as we gathered in his arms and felt the campfire and the repetition and fell asleep. My grandpa Al was a wise man. He put us virtually in the warmth of the fire and in the warmth of his never finished story until we fell asleep blessed by his wisdom and his company and his version of prayer.

On seeing a wise person:

בָּרוּךְ אַתָּה יהוה אֱלֹהֵינוּ מֶלֶךְ הָעוֹלָם שֶׁנָּתַן מֵחָכְמָתוֹ לְבָשָׂר וָדָם:

Barukh ata Adonay eloheynu melekh ha'olam shenatan mechokhmato l'vasar v'dam.

Blessed are you, Eternal One our God, the sovereign of all worlds who has bestowed upon mortals some of your wisdom.

IN A MARKET-DRIVEN SOCIETY that valorizes youth, elders are often seen as behind the times. Most advertising is not aimed at them. Jewish tradition, by contrast, has always valued the wisdom that comes with experience, learning and age. Thus *Pirkey Avot* (wisdom of the rabbis recorded in the Mishnah during the third century) says we should rise for our elders. Take note of

—who can mentor you,

—who makes a telling comment or asks a critical question at a meeting,

—who teaches in a way that brings new insight.

Each such person is a blessing capable of starting you in a new direction. For that to happen, you need to watch and listen.

Rav came to a place where there was a drought. He decreed a fast, but the rain did not come. A prayer leader went down and said, "Who causes the wind to blow," and the wind blew. He said, "Who causes the rain to fall," and it started to rain. Rav asked, "What do you do?" The prayer leader replied, "I am a teacher of young children, and I teach the children of the poor just like the children of the rich. And whoever cannot pay, I do not take anything from them. I have a fishpond, and whoever is lazy, I bribe him with fish. I prepare it for them, and I mollify them until they come and study." (Babylonian Talmud, *Taanit* 24a) Sometimes we do not realize we are seeing a wise person. Sometimes a wise, caring teacher modestly makes no effort to be recognized as such. This would be a good blessing to recite when you realize you are in the presence of someone wise.

On seeing a Torah scholar:

בָּרוּךְ אַתָּה יהוה אֱלֹהֵינוּ מֶלֶךְ הָעוֹלָם שֶׁחָלַק מֵחָכְמָתוֹ לִירֵאָיו:

Barukh ata Adonay eloheynu melekh haʼolam shechalak mechokhmato lireʼav.

Blessed are you, Eternal One our God, the sovereign of all worlds who has imparted divine wisdom to those who revere you.

A MAN FRUSTRATED AND overwhelmed by the noise and turmoil in the little house he shared with his wife and children went to his rabbi and asked for advice. "Bring your goat into the house," said the rabbi. Soon the man was back. "That didn't help." Now bring your chickens into the house," coached the rabbi. "That didn't help either," the man sighed. "Now bring in your geese," ordered the rabbi. Before long, the man was back. "It's the worst it has ever been," he complained. "Now," urged the rabbi, "take out the goat, chickens, and geese." A few days later the man came back to thank his rabbi and smiled with contentment. "The house is so peaceful now," he proclaimed.

Who are Torah scholars? Torah itself means teaching. Perhaps Torah scholars are the ones who teach us the ways to live a good life. They are many in number, and we have encountered them through a variety of experiences and places in our lives. We encounter them in the classroom and on the pulpit. And we can see them across a dining room table or while taking a walk and sharing an idea or when we receive help to solve a problem. Our challenge is to recognize and accept their learning and open ourselves to those who may not appear to be traditional Torah scholars. To honor these wise teachers, we should listen to their words, absorb the blessing of learning with gratitude, and preserve the lesson so we have it ready when it is needed.

On seeing an unusual-looking person or animal:

בָּרוּךְ אַתָּה יהוה אֱלֹהֵינוּ מֶלֶךְ הָעוֹלָם מְשַׁנֶּה הַבְּרִיּוֹת:

Barukh ata Adonay eloheynu melekh ha'olam meshaneh habriyot.

Blessed are you, Eternal One our God, the sovereign of all worlds who creates differences among creatures.

THE HIGHEST LEVEL OF pluralism involves celebrating differences. And the number of differences is extraordinary—nationality, ethnicity, sex, orientation, gender, race, religion, political views, species, and personal appearance, to name but a few. Appreciating those who do not look or act like us grows out of a rejection of the us-versus-them approach that is part of human instinct and out of the cultivation of an attitude of inclusion. This blessing helps to cultivate that attitude.

Rabbi Eleazar son of Rabbi Simeon was coming from his teacher's house in Migdal Gedor. He was riding on his donkey by the riverside and feeling happy because he had learned much Torah. There he chanced to meet an exceedingly ugly man, who greeted him, "Peace be upon you, rabbi." Eleazar did not return his greeting but instead said to him, "Racca (empty one or good for nothing), how ugly you are! Is everyone in your town as ugly as you are?" The man replied, "I do not know, but go and tell the craftsman who made me, 'How ugly is the vessel which you have made.'" When Rabbi Eleazar realized that he had sinned, he dismounted from the donkey and prostrated himself before the man and said to him, "I submit myself to you, forgive me!" (B. Talmud, *Taanit* 20 a-b) The story goes on that the ugly man had been so insulted that he refused to forgive the learned rabbi no matter how he begged and pleaded until finally others intervened and the rabbi promised never to do such a thing again. I like to believe that we can all learn lessons in this life, change our behavior and receive forgiveness.

The Rabbis taught that one who sees crowds of people should say, "Blessed is the one who is wise in secrets," for no two people in the crowd have similar minds and no two have the same faces.

—TALMUD, *B'RAKHOT* 58A

On Seeing a Powerful Monarch or Leader:

בָּרוּךְ אַתָּה יהוה אֱלֹהֵינוּ מֶלֶךְ הָעוֹלָם שֶׁנָּתַן מִכְּבוֹדוֹ לְבָשָׂר וָדָם:

Barukh ata Adonay eloheynu melekh ha'olam shenatan mikh'vodo l'vasar vadam.

Blessed are you, Eternal One our God, the sovereign of all worlds who gave of divine glory to flesh and blood.

———————————

WHEN THE PEOPLE ISRAEL approached the prophet Samuel and asked him to appoint a king for them, Samuel warned that they were interposing an earthly authority between themselves and the Monarch of Heaven and Earth. Nonetheless, ancient Israel had its kings. The temporal power and authority that national leaders embody does help create stability and inspire support.

Of all the rich images in the Book of Esther, the one that I remember best involves Mordecai, who saved the king's life by discovering plotters and turning them in. The king had Mordecai dressed in royal finery and driven through town by Haman, the one who despised him, while heralds announced, "Thus shall be done to the man that the king delights to honor." This delightful image conveys the significance of genuine leaders.

What do we do when there is no fanfare announcing the arrival of a powerful leader or monarch? How do we recognize them? Some cultures and customs offer clear rituals that require respect and attention. Subjects of monarchies bow, and in military cultures, salutes and standing are required as signals of respect, as they often are for elders or people we love regardless of age. Not so very long ago, when a rabbi entered the room, all those present would rise out of respect. Such is done for people whom we wish to honor and respect!

Upon donning eyeglasses or perceiving something new:

בָּרוּךְ אַתָּה יהוה אֱלֹהֵינוּ מֶלֶךְ הָעוֹלָם פּוֹקֵחַ עִוְרִים:

Barukh ata Adonay eloheynu melekh ha'olam poke'ach ivrim.

Blessed are you, Eternal One our God, the sovereign of all worlds who opens the eyes of the blind.

WHEN I WAS IN third grade, I was reading poorly. Everything was a blur for me, so I assumed it was like that for everyone. But my teacher sent me to have my eyes tested. With my new glasses, the blur suddenly disappeared. And I have been an avid reader ever since. Every morning when I put on my glasses, I appreciate that I can see what is before me.

I have a particular weakness for kids who wear glasses. Perhaps it is because I was eight when I got my first pair. We took the bus to a clinic in Chicago, and after an exam by a medical student training to be an eye surgeon and an eight-dollar payment, I got a pair of quite remarkable pink, pointed glasses. I can still recall the miracle of seeing everything clearly. Some seven years later when I was an awkward adolescent, my enterprising grandpa challenged me to earn half the money for a pair of contact lenses. I got a job at the local Woolworth's as a soda jerk at $1.10 per hour and all the tips I could smile my way, and after many months I learned several things: One, things earned by yourself are more valuable than things that are handed directly to you. Two, working at dishing out tuna salad sandwiches and ice cream sodas and making coffee and doing the dishes and smiling taught me life lessons in management that I still use. And three, my grandpa's gift of financial management far exceeded even what I could see clearly and from all angles. Now wearing different contacts, I still smile when I clean them and care for them and remember that though I have poor sight genetically, the wonder of science has given me excellent sight, with a little help from my family.

Chapter 5

Blessings for the Body

Upon wearing new clothes:

בָּרוּךְ אַתָּה יהוה אֱלֹהֵינוּ מֶלֶךְ הָעוֹלָם מַלְבִּישׁ עֲרֻמִּים:

Barukh ata Adonay eloheynu melekh haolam malbish arumim.

Blessed are you, Eternal One our God, the sovereign of all worlds who clothes the naked.

FROM THE FIRST GARMENT of leaves in the Garden of Eden till the most recent Parisian fashion, clothes have covered our nakedness, provided warmth, marked who we are, and added texture to our lives. Each new garment is a gift for the touch, for the eye, for enhancing our lives. Clothes start out spotless and without flaw. As they wear, they become repositories for memories. If they stay with us long enough, they become objects of affection and reminders of how we see ourselves. How fortunate we are that our ancestors put together those first simple garments!

Some clothes that are new to us are old to someone else, and conversely some old clothes of ours become new clothes to someone else. They are always a blessing. It is said that taking clothes from someone's wardrobe after their death is a good deed as it continues the use of their physical belongings and they become important to you. There is a now very tattered and beloved blue tee shirt that belonged to my dad. We bought it for him on a trip, and he loved it and wore it constantly. When he died, the shirt became one of my favorite hang-around shirts. Soft and worn and very much a reminder of his personality, it was new to me but old for him.

Og the Giant in three steps came from a warm climate into a cold climate. There is nothing worse than a cold giant! Og was furious, and there is little worse than a furious giant. He called for help in a giant way, and it came running in the form of the mayor in town. "I need a coat," yelled Og. And the mayor set about making that happen. He called for all the tailors in town to make a coat for Og the Giant. Now tailors are very competitive, and they generally do not come together to sew, but this time they put pride aside, and they all brought pieces of fabric and thread, as no one had enough to clothe Og's large frame. They worked through the night and then another and came up with a colorful patchwork coat they presented to Og. So exhausted were they that they fell asleep in one of the pockets of his new coat. Og put the coat on and sighed with relief at his warmth and looked around to thank the tailors who were either asleep in his pocket or cowering in fear at his potential wrath. He found them, and with one very large hand he pulled them out and held them gently there and said, "Thank you." Had he known how, Og would certainly have added this blessing.

Upon awakening:

בָּרוּךְ אַתָּה יהוה אֱלֹהֵינוּ מֶלֶךְ הָעוֹלָם הַמַּעֲבִיר שֵׁנָה מֵעֵינַי וּתְנוּמָה מֵעַפְעַפָּי:

Barukh ata Adonay eloheynu melekh ha'olam hama'avir shena me'eynay ut'numa me'afapay.

Blessed are you, Eternal One our God, the sovereign of all worlds who removes sleep from my eyes and slumber from my eyelids.

FALLING ASLEEP IS AN act of faith because while we are asleep, we are completely out of control. Sleep restores and renews us in both body and mind, so that faith is critical to our wellbeing. Awakening brings our minds back into conscious activity. We are again ready to embrace life.

The rabbis tell a story about Adam and the coming of the first night of his life. How was he to know that the darkness he was experiencing for the first time would ever end? He must have been terrified, and who knows if Adam and Eve were capable of comforting each other, having just met. The philosopher Bertrand Russell reminds us that the assumption that the sun will rise tomorrow, while certainly reasonable based on past experience, is never absolutely certain. So we have to rely on what we've seen so far. Imagine, therefore, poor Adam; he had no experience at all, and on that first night God did not tuck him in with such a promise. And then he awoke!

Waking in the morning and reciting its blessings can be the most passionate, the most grateful, and the most hopeful moment of the day. Those of us who don't sleep well at night, who lie awake thinking about all that we have to do tomorrow or all that we didn't finish today, know about chaos and order. It is helpful to know that there will be a tomorrow; it is really helpful to know that there will be many tomorrows (although, with sadness, we acknowledge the pain of those who know that they have but few tomorrows). Many of the morning blessings are about putting our personal day in order and reassuring ourselves about the continuity of creation, with its infinite number of days.

This is the day that God has made—let us rejoice in it.

—PSALMS 118:24

When freed from a physical or spiritual constraint:

בָּרוּךְ אַתָּה יהוה אֱלֹהֵינוּ מֶלֶךְ הָעוֹלָם מַתִּיר אֲסוּרִים:

Barukh ata Adonay eloheynu melekh ha'olam matir asurim.

Blessed are you, Eternal One our God, the sovereign of all worlds who frees the captive.

WHEN I THINK ABOUT being bound, slavery and incarceration are what usually comes to mind. But we are also constrained by injury, illness, and physical and mental disability. Coming back to full strength and full freedom of movement can provide an exhilarating sense of relief. Another time to give thanks!

On the 50th Anniversary of the March on Selma, I told an interactive story at a professional development conference for early childhood educators. I was teaching the educators how to use stories and puppets to engage their students in the upward battle to literacy. The story we told together is called the "Kingdom of the Singing Birds." It is a wonderful tale built on the Rabbi Zusya line that says, "It is not up to you to do as your father did but as you should do."

In the story the wise woman helps the Queen find a way to make the birds that live in an amazing aviary sing. They had lived in that aviary in the time of her mother the Queen and her grandmother the Queen, and they had never sung. After a series of questions to a variety of people and many failed attempts to make the birds sing, she goes to see the wise woman for her advice. The wise woman recommends that if she wants the birds to sing, she must set them free. The Queen says, "Why should I do as my mother didn't do and as my grandmother didn't do?" The wise woman tells her, "The answer is not that you should do as your mother or your grandmother did, but as you should do. If you want your birds to sing, you must set them free."

And so she does, and of course they begin to sing.

It is an extremely effective story on many levels. It is interactive and strong, and that is usually enough. However on this day when the keynote was over and I was cleaning up, an African American woman came up to me and thanked me for telling and teaching that story and for reminding the gathered community of that historical event. She said, "If it weren't for that day, I wouldn't be here."

When able to stand straight or free oneself of a burden:

בָּרוּךְ אַתָּה יהוה אֱלֹהֵינוּ מֶלֶךְ הָעוֹלָם זוֹקֵף כְּפוּפִים:

Barukh ata Adonay eloheynu melekh haʾolam zokef kʾfufim.

Blessed are you, Eternal One our God, the sovereign of all worlds who raises up the humble.

MANY THINGS CAN CAUSE us to slump—a playground bully, a bad back-ache, a harsh boss, the disapproval of peers, poor physical condition. How wonderful it is when healing occurs and relationships improve, how wonderful to stand tall once again!

There is a lot to be learned by watching how a person stands, walks and sits. Some of that is easy to see: a person leaning over in pain or someone recovering from an accident, for example. But those are not the character-istics I am thinking about. I am writing about body image and body lan-guage. We unwittingly use our bodies to speak our moods. A person who is fearful will invariably slouch and even bend over to appear smaller. People who are embarrassed by their bodies might cover themselves up with flow-ing robes or keep their heads down, eyes lowered. Generally the message is clear if one is paying attention. The outside world might notice, but often people are oblivious to the message conveyed by their own posture and attire. When we are walking or sitting, our stances can even express things we might not feel. Walking as tall and erect as we can presents us as if we were not burdened or fearful. When we become confident-appearing, the world reacts to us differently. An interesting experiment that I've tried with students is to have them slouch with their heads down and backs slumped. Then I ask them how they feel. Invariably they feel sad, tired and uncom-fortable. Then we continue with the opposite. When the students' heads are up and their backs are straight, they say they feel stronger, more confident and surer of themselves. When we stand straight, we are less of a burden to ourselves and everyone else.

In appreciation of the satisfaction of physical needs:

בָּרוּךְ אַתָּה יהוה אֱלֹהֵינוּ מֶלֶךְ הָעוֹלָם שֶׁעָשָׂה לִי כָּל־צָרְכִּי:

Barukh ata Adonay eloheynu melekh ha'olam she'asa li kol tzorki.

Blessed are you, Eternal One our God, the sovereign of all worlds who has satisfied all my needs.

UNLIKE MOST BLESSINGS, THIS one is written in the past tense. In the present moment, most of us focus on what is not yet complete or not quite right. That criticism often leads us to act, but no sooner do we finish resolving one issue than we start to focus on the next. Only with the benefit of hindsight can most of us see that our needs were indeed met. Our day-to-day complaints disappear when we look across the years and realize how much we have actually received.

I realize that lately I've been thinking more about my faith than about the dimensions of my hips. As for my hips, they were an issue, but then they became a blessing as a shelf that I carted a child around on, and eventually they became an important place to rest my hands as I looked sternly at an unruly audience. Hips widen—no big deal. But the effort to keep them in check has become more difficult as time passes. Granted this is not a complaint. I put some work in on the battle, but then along came Avery, my first grandchild, and my hips came into important use again for carrying, snuggling, and other grandmotherly activities. They remain my personal protrusions.

On the other hand the same is true of my faith, my spirit. I seem to have more of it, not less, as the years go by. It increases in my head and my heart. I believe that I've been more successful at achieving peace in my head and my heart because of it. Things that used to bother me bother me less, and situations that made me anxious are far less distressing.

So what is to be surmised by the similarity of these two different aspects of my life, the physical and the psychic parts of myself, my hips and my faith? I don't mean to make light (isn't that a witty reference) of either of these phenomena. Perhaps or "per<u>hips</u>" I should use my new calm to smile at the mirror instead of frown and be grateful for this additional gift of faith that the important parts of my life are in good shape if not even a tad more curvy. And not forget to thank God.

On getting a second wind:

בָּרוּךְ אַתָּה יהוה אֱלֹהֵינוּ מֶלֶךְ הָעוֹלָם הַנּוֹתֵן לַיָּעֵף כֹּחַ:

Barukh ata Adonay eloheynu melekh ha'olam hanoten laya'ef ko'ach.

Blessed are you, Eternal One our God, the sovereign of all worlds who gives strength to the weary.

———————————————

WHEN I STAY UP too late, getting up is hard. During an intense day, my energy declines, and I am grateful for a second wind. When a hike turns out to be longer than I expected, I am surprised to feel a late surge of energy. When my kids were young, I needed that infusion after their bedtime, when I turned back to my desk. Strength does come to the weary.

Many years ago it was important for me and a friend to walk 39 miles to complete an Avon walk to raise money for breast cancer research. 39 miles is a long way to walk. About halfway through we were tired from our heads to our toes, but we found inspiration in the conversations about survivors and non-survivors of that disease. We told stories, sang songs and pushed ourselves forward to complete our goal. We had more than one second wind. We each find strength in our own way. Some people drink a cup of coffee, others seek out an engaging conversation, a nap, or a run. The trick is to understand your own weariness and based on that, find a way to give yourself strength. We particularly gain strength when we are doing something we know has to be done. Our obligations, passions and curiosity drive us, but that second wind also comes from a source outside ourselves. I call it God.

In appreciation of the capacity to act:

בָּרוּךְ אַתָּה יהוה אֱלֹהֵינוּ מֶלֶךְ הָעוֹלָם שֶׁעָשַׂנִי בֶּן / בַּת־חוֹרִין:

Barukh ata Adonay eloheynu melekh ha'olam she'asani ben/bat chorin.

Blessed are you, Eternal One our God, the sovereign of all worlds who has made me free.

MY LIFE IS FILLED with choices, an uncountable number over the course of a day. Should I hit the snooze alarm? What shall I wear? Do I need a haircut? The choices range from totally trivial to life-changing. Being free gives us opportunities for shaping our relationships, our conduct, our futures.

Internal factors can prevent us from acting freely. Fear, avoidance of the unknown, and the inability to accept change can hold us captive. Like the classic train from *The Little Engine That Could* who took on an enormous challenge rejected by bigger trains that were too busy or too important or too old, we can conquer our internal resistance and do what we thought we could not. That little blue engine gave us words that can free us to do our part. "I think I can, I think I can!" As the engine got over the mountain, she said, "I thought I could, I thought I could." The engine was ready to say this blessing.

> Pride in our wisdom and good deeds should induce us to increase them and make use of them, and that should lead to humility through gratitude for these precious abilities.
>
> —BAHYA IBN PAKUDA, *DUTIES OF THE HEART* 34.5

After recovering from an illness or injury:

בָּרוּךְ אַתָּה יהוה רוֹפֵא כָל בָּשָׂר וּמַפְלִיא לַעֲשׂוֹת:

Barukh ata Adonay eloheynu melekh haʾolam rofeh khol basar umafli laʾasot.

Blessed are you, Eternal One our God, the sovereign of all worlds who wondrously heals all flesh.

BEING A BIT CLUMSY, I have had more than my share of scraped knees and elbows, bruises, and broken bones, to say nothing of allergy attacks. I am grateful when the pain goes away, and I continue to be amazed by the way new skin grows under the scabs, the bones knit, headaches recede. We can heal, regain strength, return to full activity. We ourselves are wonders.

A while back a friend recovered from a serious heart attack. Through the constant professional medical care and diligent work of the patient himself, he recovered and is healthy today. After his illness and recovery, I saw his wife and asked how he was doing. I don't know what particular button I pushed. I do know that she was able to talk to me because I was her friend. She turned and tearfully said. "Nobody ever asks me how I am doing. Why is that?" She was tired and anxious. Although the ultimate goal of his recovery had been achieved, she was left with a weariness that most did not notice. It was an extremely important lesson for me. People don't recover by themselves, yet few of us notice that when the task is finished, the caregivers should be blessed as well. Only with their partnership does the work of healing get done.

Why is God described as doing wonders? Because people are like balloons full of air. Making a hole the size of a needlepoint in a balloon causes the air to escape. Human beings are full of openings, and their air is still preserved inside them. This is a wonder! Just as remarkable is the way the body picks out the good from food we eat and rejects the waste. —*Shulchan Arukh, Orach Chayim* 6.2

When rinsing the hands prior to eating or praying:

בָּרוּךְ אַתָּה יהוה אֱלֹהֵינוּ מֶלֶךְ הָעוֹלָם אֲשֶׁר קִדְּשָׁנוּ בְּמִצְוֹתָיו וְצִוָּנוּ עַל נְטִילַת יָדָיִם:

Barukh ata Adonay eloheynu melekh ha'olam asher kid'shanu b'mitzvotav vetzivanu al n'tilat yadayim.

Blessed are you, Eternal One our God, the sovereign of all worlds who has made us holy with your mitzvot and commanded us to wash our hands.

IN THE DAYS WHEN the ancient Temple (*Bet Hamikdash*) stood in Jerusalem, the priests were required to wash their hands prior to offering sacrifices. With the Temple destroyed, the early rabbis transferred that ritual to every Jew, with the idea that every home can be a *mikdash m'at,* a small sanctuary. When we wash and then break bread, we are in the role of the priests, dedicating our meals to Divine service.

There are few people reading these words who have not heard the request to wash their hands before they eat. This blessing is not about that request. This is a much more self-conscious form of washing than the physical cleansing of one's hands. This spiritual washing honors the meal we are about to begin and turns the table into an altar. On Shabbat the hand-washing blessing comes between the Kiddush and the motzi, and it is a lovely tradition not to speak after washing until the motzi is said and bread is eaten. I have strong memories of this silence at camp and the ways in which people honor this silence. It is a moment for reflection usually accompanied by quietly going to the table and smiling at the rest of the people, waiting for everyone to be ready, and then saying the blessing. It takes hand washing to a new and prayerful place, making the everyday holy.

Chapter 6

Blessings for Shabbat and Holidays

For Shabbat:

בָּרוּךְ אַתָּה יהוה אֱלֹהֵינוּ מֶלֶךְ הָעוֹלָם מְקַדֵּשׁ הַשַּׁבָּת:

Barukh ata Adonay eloheynu melekh ha'olam m'kadesh hashabbat.

Blessed are you, Eternal One our God, the sovereign of all worlds who sets apart Shabbat.

IT IS A STRUGGLE in our contemporary world to find time for focusing on gratitude, for being rather than doing, for reflection and celebration instead of producing and consuming. Shabbat is a time set apart for precisely those purposes. Shabbat sanctifies our lives when we dedicate time to Shabbat.

The hustle and bustle of the workweek caused her considerable stress. She often rushed into Shabbat, bringing that stress with her. One Friday, late afternoon left her more frantic than usual, and she snapped and grumbled at everyone in her path on the way home. The final straw came when she discovered that she had forgotten her keys at the office and couldn't get in the front door or the side door or any other accessible entry. She sat on the front steps and began to cry. As in many stories, someone appeared as if out of nowhere and asked what was wrong. And as in many stories, once the flood of emotions and complaints was over, she calmed down and found herself telling her story to someone she didn't know. Lost in conversation, she discovered relief and then gratitude for the letting go. It might even have been at that moment that she found she actually did have her keys, or that her partner or housemate or kid came by with one and let her into the house. It might have ended with any of those things, making her passage into Shabbat easier. She let go and moved forward, leaving the angst behind.

When she turned around to thank the stranger, no one was there.

A personal practice that someone taught me years ago is to call people in my world that I wanted to particularly wish a sweet Shabbat. Some calls included people that I don't regularly see, and some calls were people that I see regularly. One rabbi friend calls her grown children right before Shabbat and blesses them on the phone.

When lighting Shabbat candles:

בָּרוּךְ אַתָּה יהוה אֱלֹהֵינוּ מֶלֶךְ הָעוֹלָם אֲשֶׁר קִדְּשָׁנוּ בְּמִצְוֹתָיו וְצִוָּנוּ לְהַדְלִיק נֵר שֶׁל שַׁבָּת:

Barukh ata Adonay eloheynu melekh ha'olam asher kid'shanu b'mitzvotav vetzivanu l'hadlik ner shel Shabbat.

Blessed are you, Eternal One our God, the sovereign of all worlds who has made us holy with your mitzvot and commanded us to kindle Shabbat light.

IN PREMODERN TIMES, THE candles lit at sunset provided the light for Shabbat dinner. The candles' glow no longer provides most of the brightness in our households, but that soft glow warms the room and brightens our hearts when we let the light shine in.

A certain calm and order begins when the Shabbat candles are lit. Their gentle flame marks the time of rest and creative order in our personal universe. Hans Christian Anderson often wrote stories where everyday objects were his spokesmen. One of his stories features candles, and I tell a version of it on Shabbat. Anderson's story tells of two candles, one of tallow and one of beeswax. The more expensive beeswax candle, saved for special occasions, tells of how excited it is to be lighting the hall for a formal party that night. The tallow candle, envious of that glitter and joy, responds that it wishes it were possible to go to a party, see the beautiful gowns, and hear the wonderful music. That night right before the party, the tallow candle is given to the house's servant woman along with some extra, special food for her good work during the day with all the extra preparation for the event. She gratefully packs all of it into her bag and takes it home to her children, who delight in the food and revel in the stories she tells them by the tallow candle's light. She is then able to continue her work through the night because of the candle's glow. On reflection the tallow candle is struck by how its gift of light has brought so much joy. When we kindle the Shabbat candles to separate the workweek from our special day, the candle is a wonderful gift to be blessed.

On ending Shabbat or a holiday:

בָּרוּךְ אַתָּה יהוה אֱלֹהֵינוּ מֶלֶךְ הָעוֹלָם הַמַּבְדִיל בֵּין קֹדֶשׁ לְחוֹל:

Barukh ata Adonay eloheynu melekh ha'olam hamavdil beyn kodesh l'chol.

Blessed are you, Eternal One our God, the sovereign of all worlds who separates the holy from the ordinary.

A JEWISH TRADITION TEACHES that on Shabbat we have an extra soul, *neshama y'tera*. That helps us to encounter the peace and holiness of Shabbat. But Shabbat is only special in contrast to the rest of the week, which is filled with work of all sorts. That is one reason why even the wealthiest people are required to do some of the household Shabbat preparation themselves. Without the contrast between work and rest, Shabbat would have no meaning. As Shabbat (or a holiday) gives way to the beginning of the workweek, we express gratitude both for the holy and for the everyday, for each gives meaning to the other.

The ceremony of Havdalah, separation, traditionally brings Shabbat to closure. The ceremony is filled with a glorious array for the senses. We light a candle when Shabbat is officially over, smell the pungent and sweet fragrances, such as cloves or rosemary; sip the wine; and then use it to squelch the flame of the candle. The ceremony uses all of our senses and prepares us to return to the week refreshed and invigorated. The assembled wish each other "Shavua Tov—a good week," and the separation is complete. This is also a good time to bid farewell to Elijah the prophet, who I like to believe has been with us for the 25 hours of Shabbat, as it is his time to move on as well.

It was the custom in one town that whenever there was a party, everyone in town was invited. Just as the dinner party was about to begin, there was a knock on the door. When the host answered, there stood a man in torn garments. He seemed like a beggar, so of course the host said he could come in but must enter through the kitchen and eat there as well, and then he closed the door. Minutes later there was another knock on the door, and a man with an elegant suit and tie stood there. Of course the host ushered him in and seated him to the right of the host. The meal was served course by course, conversation was lively, and all was preceded with the appropriate blessings. But after each course, the elegantly garbed man would take the food that he was given and put it in various pockets of his clothes. The salad went in his vest pocket, the cold soup in his jacket pocket, the fish course in another, and so on until the people could stand it no longer. They demanded to know why he was so disrespectful to his host at this very fine feast. He had a clear answer which he delivered standing in front them with a leaf of lettuce trailing out of his pants pocket. "You see," he said, "When I knocked on the door dressed as a beggar, I was sent to the kitchen. But when I came back dressed in fine clothes, I was invited in. I therefore thought you were more interested in feeding my clothes than in feeding me." Then Elijah moved on. May you be blessed with the power to see past appearances to the image of God in each person you encounter this week.

On entering a Sukkah:

בָּרוּךְ אַתָּה יהוה אֱלֹהֵינוּ מֶלֶךְ הָעוֹלָם אֲשֶׁר קִדְּשָׁנוּ בְּמִצְוֹתָיו וְצִוָּנוּ לֵישֵׁב בַּסֻּכָּה:

Barukh ata Adonay eloheynu melekh haʼolam asher kidʼshanu bʼmitzvotav vetzivanu leyshev basuka.

Blessed are you, Eternal One our God, the sovereign of all worlds who has made us holy with your mitzvot and commanded us to dwell in the sukkah.

THE TEMPORARY DWELLING OF the sukkah lets in the world outside—the wind, rain, hot, cold, sun, and stars. We create a bright and loving atmosphere while experiencing the elements. In the fragility of the sukkah we are reminded that the elements are far more powerful than even the sturdiest of buildings. Loving relationships can shield us from the most powerful of storms.

I have been in many sukkahs, from rooftop ones in the city of New York to ones that grace a *bimah* in a synagogue to a most fabulous one made from a grape arbor so that you could reach up and have a nosh while visiting. It is rare that the weather is perfect but also rare that the mood is not festive with or without chattering teeth. A sukkah is a temporary home and a great visual aid for kids who, like me, need to see to learn. One of the most striking memories I have of entering a sukkah came because of who was invited to come in with me. Of course we usually fill the sukkah with earthly guests. A tradition known as *Ushpizin* (Aramaic for guests) calls upon us to welcome in seven spiritual guests from our biblical past as well: Abraham, Isaac, Jacob, Moses, Aaron, Joseph, and David. Contemporary versions of *Ushpizin* invite biblical women alongside the men. There are many people who can no longer sit with us under the Sukkah, but we can bring them in by hanging their pictures. We can also invite the people that we love by adding them to the traditional list of *Ushpizins*.

We come out of our homes filled with all sorts of goodness and dwell in sukkot right after the harvest to remember that the Israelites had no inheritance in the wilderness and no houses to inhabit. Thus we give thanks for our inheritance and our houses full of goodness, and we do not say, "We achieved this solely by the work of our hands."

—Rashbam on *Leviticus* 23:43

Chapter 7

Blessings for Special Occasions

Upon reaching a major milestone:

בָּרוּךְ אַתָּה יהוה אֱלֹהֵינוּ מֶלֶךְ הָעוֹלָם שֶׁהֶחֱיָנוּ וְקִיְּמָנוּ וְהִגִּיעָנוּ לַזְּמַן הַזֶּה:

Barukh ata Adonay eloheynu melekh ha'olam shehecheyanu v'kiy'manu v'higiyanu laz'man hazeh.

Blessed are you, Eternal One our God, the sovereign of all worlds who gave us life, and kept us strong, and brought us to this time.

EVEN WHEN DAILY LIVING seems like a grind, there are moments that uplift us—a birthday, holiday, bar/t mitzvah, graduation, family reunion or birth. Reaching the milestone, and often sharing it with others, can bring joy, elation, a sense of connection, of grace that moves us beyond the ordinary. Such a moment provides an ideal opportunity for a blessing that helps us to savor the gift of the moment.

This blessing is used on many joyous occasions, including birthdays, first fruits of the season, and new babies. It is recited at so many ceremonies and celebrations that there are some people who search out *shehecheyanu* moments. There is one time I use this blessing that always makes me smile—when I say it after seeing a friend I haven't seen in more than 30 days. When I was young, I lived in walking distance from my grandparents, so I saw them often. But now it is different. Many children live a plane ride or a long drive away from family. There are many other reasons besides distance that we miss seeing our loved ones and friends. Someone may have been sick or away on business or just have a jammed schedule. This blessing is one of reconnection, thanking God for getting us to this point where we are again in the presence of those we cherish.

When experiencing gratitude:

בָּרוּךְ אַתָּה יהוה אֱלֹהֵינוּ מֶלֶךְ הָעוֹלָם הַטּוֹב שִׁמְךָ וּלְךָ נָאֶה לְהוֹדוֹת:

Barukh ata Adonay eloheynu melekh ha'olam hatov shim'kha ul'kha na'eh l'hodot.

Blessed are you, Eternal One our God, the sovereign of all worlds whose name is Good and to whom it is good to give thanks.

"I DID IT MYSELF" is a sensible exclamation when uttered by someone who just tied her shoes on her own for the first time. But even that first would not have happened without someone teaching her how to tie a bow. As Albert Einstein once explained, "I stand on the shoulders of giants." So do we all. Giving thanks for our good fortune is a valuable first step in passing it forward.

When little kids are excited to see you, they visibly shiver with excitement. I have been fortunate to experience that joy, and I hope you have as well. Some thanks, of course, are quieter. They can be in the form of a smile or a hug or a beautifully expressed hand-written note. Regardless of the outer form, gratitude comes from within us. In many places in the *Tanakh* (Hebrew Bible) we read of the earth-shaking experience of gratitude. Here are two examples:

> Let the sea roar in its fullness;
> The world, and all who dwell on it.
> Let the floods clap their hands;
> Let the mountains join in singing for joy.

> —PSALMS 98:7–8

> For you will go out with joy,
> And go forth in peace;
> The mountains and hills will break forth in song before you,
> And all the trees of the field shall clap their hands.

> —ISAIAH 55:12

Upon hearing good news:

בָּרוּךְ אַתָּה יהוה אֱלֹהֵינוּ מֶלֶךְ הָעוֹלָם הַטּוֹב וְהַמֵּטִיב לַכֹּל:

Barukh ata Adonay eloheynu melekh ha'olam hatov v'hametiv lakol.

Blessed are you, Eternal One our God, the sovereign of all worlds who is good and does good for all.

WE HUMANS ARE FRAGILE creatures living in a world where there is much that is beyond our control. I can eat well and exercise, but I have no control over my genes or storms or random crimes. We cling to our illusion of control, but we know that our lives could change at any moment. Some of what comes our way is wonderful news—the birth of a child, the end of a war or successful surgery, to name but a few of the possibilities. This blessing gives us a chance to mark these moments of grace that come from beyond us.

It is a Jewish custom to accept good news in many ways. There is the traditional mazel tov—interpreted as "Congratulations!" There is *"Barukh hashem,"* blessing God's name while putting the good news in God's arena. There is my grandmother's superstitious custom of spitting—*poo poo poo*—so that the ever-present "evil one" won't hear of the good news and come to make trouble; those with good news are thereby kept safe. Some knock on wood from a Christian custom referring to the crucifix, and the list goes on. Yet some things are universal. When good news is delivered, it is generally welcomed with a smile, often a tear, a hug, and usually a feeling that travels deep inside, making an impact that is hard to describe. Perhaps it is where Elijah waits, perhaps it is where God listens, perhaps it is the beginning of a story you are waiting to tell—because all storytellers work hard to have good endings and happily-ever-afters! Recognizing the source of good fortune brings joy all by itself.

> Rabbi Hanina Bar Pappa said, "When someone derives enjoyment from this world without offering a blessing, it is tantamount to stealing from God."
>
> —TALMUD, *B'RAKHOT* 35A

When honoring newlyweds:

בָּרוּךְ אַתָּה יהוה אֱלֹהֵינוּ מֶלֶךְ הָעוֹלָם מְשַׂמֵּחַ חָתָן וְכַלָּה:

Barukh ata Adonay eloheynu melekh ha'olam m'same'ach chatan v'khala.

Blessed are you, Eternal One our God, the sovereign of all worlds who causes bride and groom to rejoice.

THE RABBIS OF THE Talmud were concerned about telling the truth. Hillel said that we should always tell a bride she is beautiful. Shammai demurred, saying that only a beautiful bride should be told that. What was Hillel thinking? Perhaps that the inner glow and joy of a bride make her beautiful regardless of the details of her physical appearance.

Jewish custom dictates seven nights of celebration following a wedding. Rather than disappearing on a honeymoon, couples following that tradition are buoyed each night by friends, family, and community joining together to rejoice with bride and groom.

Under the *hupah*, the marriage canopy, at our daughter's wedding, the rabbi spoke of what the *hupah* meant to him and symbolically for the Jewish community. He described it as the home, a place where one could be safe and able to find personal sanctuary, shelter, and peace. The non-Jewish father of the groom listened with great interest, and at the end of this Jewish ceremony that was totally unfamiliar to him, he remained standing under the *hupah*. The father of the bride noticed his absence among the milling, noisy guests and quietly went back and asked him if he was all right. "Yes," he responded. "I thought I'd stay here for a while because the rabbi said I'd be safe here." Then he smiled and entered the fray. He danced with his wife and then the bride, and became one with the new community.

FROM GRATITUDE TO BLESSINGS AND BACK

When holding your newborn for the first time:

בָּרוּךְ אַתָּה יהוה אֱלֹהֵינוּ מֶלֶךְ הָעוֹלָם מְשַׂמֵּחַ הָאֵם בִּפְרִי בִטְנָה וּמַגִיל הָאָב בְּיוֹצֵא חֲלָצָיו:

Barukh ata Adonay eloheynu melekh ha'olam m'same'ach ha'em bifri vitna umagil ha'av b'yotzey chalatzav.

Blessed are you, Eternal One our God, the sovereign of all worlds who lets the mother rejoice in the fruit of her womb and the father with his offspring.

MANY PEOPLE SAY THAT the moment of holding their newborns for the first time gave them the strongest sense of miracle and transcendence that they have ever experienced. The gift of life underlines the joyous mystery in which all of us participate. The gift of a child draws us further into a life of love, trust, and responsibility.

This blessing explicitly invokes the mother and father of an infant, but it should not be limited to birth parents. It is expandable to include anyone who holds the infant, anyone in "the village" that will raise this child. In the best of all possible worlds, that could be a large number of people. Holding and cuddling a baby, and being delighted and overwhelmed by the possibilities that babies represent, deserves such a blessing. This blessing can also be said by the volunteers who sit in neonatal units in hospitals rocking and hugging newborn babies, for theirs is a blessed role, and the babies are blessed by their presence.

Upon hearing of a death or other bad news:

בָּרוּךְ אַתָּה יהוה אֱלֹהֵינוּ מֶלֶךְ הָעוֹלָם דַּיַּן הָאֱמֶת:

Barukh ata Adonay eloheynu melekh ha'olam dayan ha'emet.

Blessed are you, Eternal One our God, the sovereign of all worlds, the true judge.

THERE IS NO WAY to outlive death, so most of the time we pretend that is not our final end. Jewish tradition takes death as a given. Mourning rituals are not tucked away. They are in the home and the community where everyone—young and old—encounters them. Every death we hear about is a foreshadowing of our own deaths, and it is a reminder of everyone we have lost in the past. Acknowledging a death is also an acknowledgment that no person has ultimate control.

The realization that one is dying brings out untested skills in reflection for most people. I was the recipient of the journal and reflections of my friend Joe. The journal beautifully describes a saga that starts with reflections of his early growing up in southern Indiana and continues with a variety of escapades of a gay, talented man who died of AIDS at the age of 45. Many of his lessons were personal to me, and much of his legacy was to bring the arts to our community with a little help from his friends. Joseph believed that the arts and love could bring calm to the world. He made a lot of that happen. In 1992 when he was diagnosed with AIDS, there was no cure, so although he never addressed it, he knew that he was dying. The following is his reflection on death:

"As I get older, the questions multiply, and the answers become more elusive. I look back on 43 years of what must be a very average life on this planet of billions and find that it has all been an incredible gift. And yet I am greedy. I want more of it as I have come to ponder my mortality, and the real darkness that death might mean. But perhaps it isn't death that stops our journey. Maybe it is stopping our journey that brings death."

Chapter 8

Other Blessings

After praying:

בָּרוּךְ אַתָּה יהוה אֱלֹהֵינוּ מֶלֶךְ הָעוֹלָם שׁוֹמֵעַ תְּפִלָּה:

Barukh ata Adonay eloheynu melekh ha'olam shome'a t'fila.

Blessed are you, Eternal One our God, the sovereign of all worlds who hears prayer.

SOMETIMES I PRAY ALONE, sometimes with a group. Some of the prayers are silent or spoken softly, and others are sung aloud. I don't pray for God's benefit; God does not depend upon my prayers. The one person who most needs to hear my prayer is I. "My God, the soul You put in me is pure." "Keep me from speaking evil." "May there be peace in the world." And what part of me is most affected by my prayer? The part that is *b'tzelem Elohim*, in the image of God. Prayer brings me to the Divine within, and I pray for that part of myself to guide me through my days. God, hear my prayer.

I'm a prayer, one who prays. Not so one would notice, but it is always on my mind if not spoken out loud. I attribute some of it to my awareness of the wonders that surround us and some because I have a strong belief that I am not solely responsible for anything I do. Some call it luck, good fortune or hard work, and all of those things are in part true. I am constantly reminding myself that some thanks need to be given, and that is where my prayers come in. It might take the form of talking to God. No answers are expected. Then there are the times when I go to pray in community. Often it is hard to program, plan or just plain get myself there. It's a bit like working out, it is often difficult to get myself to go to the gym, but I force myself to go, and I always feel good afterward. So it is with services. The second I enter the room and am surrounded by the community in prayer, it again comes together for me. Prayer comes in many forms. Yesterday at Shabbat services, two sisters (combined age 198) sat in front of me and slowly but steadily joined in prayer. When a mensch brought them shawls because he knew they got cold, there too was prayer. When we joined together in song and silence and Torah discussions and wrapped ourselves in tallitot and chatted over cookies, we were in prayer and God was in our conversations.

In celebration of the Jewish people:

בָּרוּךְ אַתָּה יהוה אֱלֹהֵינוּ מֶלֶךְ הָעוֹלָם אוֹהֵב עַמּוֹ יִשְׂרָאֵל:

Barukh ata Adonay eloheynu melekh ha'olam ohev amo Yisrael.

Blessed are you, Eternal One our God, the sovereign of all worlds who loves the people Israel.

WHEN WE FEEL FULLY loved, we have no urge to compete with others for who is the most loved. Proclaiming Israel as beloved of God is not comparative. It only celebrates that Jews experience Divine love refracted through Jewish tradition.

There were two kids whose favorite argument, in jest or not, was who mom loved more. They spent an unhealthy amount of time debating the issue and trying to prove their points. Their demonstrations were clever and interesting examples of why their mother should choose one over the other. I imagine there are few households that don't have those arguments when there is more than one child in the family. I know that it was the case when I raised my family, and now I see it in the household where my grandchildren are being raised. It is endemic, frustrating and eternal! This can also be the argument about a sovereign who loves all people. We bless the Eternal our God who loves the people Israel and are grateful for that love, but we also recognize that the sovereign of all worlds loves all individuals and all peoples, and we are grateful to be in their company. Love from most moms and from God is unlimited.

When beginning Jewish study or listening to Jewish teaching:

בָּרוּךְ אַתָּה יהוה אֱלֹהֵינוּ מֶלֶךְ הָעוֹלָם אֲשֶׁר קִדְּשָׁנוּ בְּמִצְוֹתָיו וְצִוָּנוּ לַעֲסוֹק בְּדִבְרֵי תוֹרָה:

Barukh ata Adonay eloheynu melekh ha'olam asher kid'shanu b'mitzvotav vetzivanu la'asok b'divrey Torah.

Blessed are you, Eternal One our God, the sovereign of all worlds who has made us holy with your mitzvot and commanded us to engage in words of Torah.

———————————————————

JEWISH TRADITION TEACHES THAT God's love is manifest in Torah. Perhaps that is why Torah study leads to contemplating the meaning in life and the best way to live. Sacred study is not so much about acquiring knowledge as it is about gaining wisdom. Fulfilling the mitzvah of Jewish learning is meant to deepen our awareness and strengthen our commitment to virtue. Those concerns can help us decide what we want to study.

After his parents taught their son at home for his first five years, it was time to send him off to study in town with boys and girls his own age and with people who might know more than his parents. He was frightened and worried about many things. Would they like him? Would he be able to keep up? Would his parents miss him while he was gone, and would they be able to get along without him? He had already learned much of the *aleph bet* as individual letters, and now his excitement that the letters would be put together chased some, but not all, of his fears away. What if he forgot the letters?

On his first day of *heder* (school) as he was about to leave with his *abba* (father), his mother put a package in his pocket to eat on the way to school, which was three miles away. As they were walking along and as he became more and more nervous, his *abba* reminded him that he had something special in his jacket pocket. He reached in and pulled out a cookie in the shape of one of the Hebrew letters! Nibbling all the way to school, he knew that he would remember and that his learning would be sweet, and so his Jewish study began.

After resolving a conflict or disagreement:

בָּרוּךְ אַתָּה יהוה אֱלֹהֵינוּ מֶלֶךְ הָעוֹלָם עֹשֶׂה הַשָּׁלוֹם:

Barukh ata Adonay eloheynu melekh ha'olam oseh hashalom.

Blessed are you, Eternal One our God, the sovereign of all worlds who makes peace.

PEACE IS OFTEN HELD as Judaism's highest value because there can only be true peace when there is also justice, sufficiency, and interpersonal caring. Overcoming conflicts with others can only be achieved by careful listening and compromise. Seeking peace requires idealism, and achieving it is impossible without self-discipline and generosity of spirit.

I picked up Avery at his theatre camp today, and we moseyed over to the Froyo store for a treat and a talk. After we ordered a dish of frozen yogurt, the friendly neighborhood Froyo clerk asked if there was anything else we wanted, and I responded as I often do, "Peace would be good." Avery added his agreement, and then we sat and munched and talked about war and death over yogurt. He wanted to know war stats and if his mama was alive during Vietnam (she was) and if his Pappy had gone to war, and if he did or didn't, why or why not. He asked good and thoughtful questions at the age of nine, and we talked about what the world would be like without war. I reminded him that although I could be helpful at my tender age of 71, chances are the good news would be won by his generation with a helping hand from ours. "Keep asking questions and don't try to make sense out of what was and move on," I reminded him and myself. We sat and ate in silence and pondered the question of who makes peace.

In recognizing our dependence on divine grace:

בָּרוּךְ אַתָּה יהוה אֲשֶׁר בְּיָדוֹ נֶפֶשׁ כָּל־חָי וְרוּחַ כָּל־בָּשָׂר:

Barukh ata Adonay eloheynu melekh ha'olam asher b'yado nefesh kol chai v'ruach kol basar.

Blessed are you, Eternal One our God, the sovereign of all worlds in whom lies the soul of every living thing and the spirit of all flesh.

HUMAN BEINGS DEPEND ON many tubes in their bodies, tubes that need to be open at some times and shut at others. Usually we take for granted that an autonomously functioning part of our brains controls all those internal passages. When we do notice the grace with which we are embodied, we recognize once again that we are surrounded by blessing.

My granddaughter Romy loves to make place cards for the dinner table. She draws them, decorates them with stickers, and carefully places and replaces them as she changes her mind about who will sit where. I save them all, and sometimes we reuse them, but mostly I keep them as a reminder of changing times and places. When people whom Romy doesn't know are invited to dinner or lunch, I have to give some description of them, including what they like, to help in the design of their place cards. Those lessons help me know the guests better as well. Recently I have been curious about where God might sit at our table and how to decoration God's place card. It would be cliched (albeit not bad) to have God as the tablecloth encompassing all of us or even as the chandelier. Does God get to sit next to Grandma, the hallowed spot, or at the head of the table smiling at all of the family? What stickers might God enjoy on the name card with one of Adonay's names? Is it glittery or fill-in-the-blanks, or does one give God all of the most cherished decorations? I think God is at the head of my table leading the blessings and smiling at my family, and I believe that Romy would enjoy decorating that name card, asking the questions she delights in asking, arguing lovingly with a God she should question and maybe even serving Adonay ice cream. Vanilla is probably God's favorite.

At the start of a meeting of a not-for-profit organization or community project:

בָּרוּךְ אַתָּה יהוה אֱלֹהֵינוּ מֶלֶךְ הָעוֹלָם אֲשֶׁר קִדְּשָׁנוּ בְּמִצְוֹתָיו וְצִוָּנוּ לַעֲסוֹק בְּצָרְכֵי צִבּוּר:

Barukh ata Adonay eloheynu melekh haʻolam asher kidʼshanu bʼmitzvotav vetzivanu laʻasok bʼtzorkhey tzibur.

Blessed are you, Eternal One our God, the sovereign of all worlds who has made us holy with your mitzvot and commanded us to engage in the needs of the community.

WHEN WE GATHER FOR a committee or board meeting, most of us think of it first as a business meeting rather than as a spiritual gathering. This blessing helps to draw the connection between organizational business and its spiritual and moral underpinnings. Abe Lincoln, the sixteenth President of the United States, was adept at making that connection by using his favorite sources—the Bible, Aesop's Fables, and Shakespeare. In his famous "Divided House" speech on June 16, 1858, he used all three. He was also known to say, "When I do good, I feel good; when I do bad, I feel bad. That's my religion." Every board and committee can use this guiding light. It is not enough for our organizations to do well. They must focus on doing good.

Upon recognizing the spiritual and moral light within oneself or others:

בָּרוּךְ אַתָּה יהוה אֱלֹהֵינוּ מֶלֶךְ הָעוֹלָם שֶׁעָשַׂנִי בְּצַלְמוֹ:

Barukh ata Adonay eloheynu melekh ha'olam she'asani b'tzalmo.

Blessed are you, Eternal One our God, the sovereign of all worlds who has made me in your image.

SEEING MYSELF AS A reflection of the Divine image helps me to strive for greater spiritual awareness and greater ethical concern. When I recognize the Divine in myself, I am more able to see it in others. And when I see it in others, it reminds to me to appreciate it in myself.

The stonecutter did not like his job. It was hot, his work cutting into the rocks was hard, and there was little glory. One day while cutting away at the stones, he saw a wealthy merchant ride by in a carriage. "Oh how I wish I were a wealthy merchant," he muttered. The moment the words left his mouth, he became a wealthy merchant! And life was good for a while. Then one day he saw the ruler of his kingdom, and the people bowed to him. "Oh," he exclaimed, "How I wish I were the king!" The moment the words came out of his month, he became the king! And life was good for a while. Then one day while he was riding in his royal chariot, the sun began to beat down on him, and he said, "Oh, the sun is much more powerful than I am. How I wish I were the sun!" The moment the words left his mouth, he became the sun. And life was good for a while. Then one day there was a rainstorm, and the clouds covered the sun, and he wished he were the clouds, as surely they were more powerful than the sun. The moment the words left his mouth, he became beautiful clouds, and he was happy for a while. Then one day the wind blew so hard that not only were the clouds blown away but so was everything in their way, except for a rock that could not be moved. So he wished he was that immovable, powerful rock. He became the rock, and he was happy for a while. Then the day came when he heard the steady and sure sound of the stonecutter, and he rejoiced that at last he had become who he was meant to be.

The stone that the builders rejected has become the chief corner-stone. This is God's doing; it is marvelous in our sight. This is the day that God has made—let us be glad and rejoice in it.

—PSALMS 118:22–24